Welcome to
JAPAN

FRANKLIN WATTS
LONDON·SYDNEY

This edition first published in 2006 by
Franklin Watts
338 Euston Road
London NW1 3BH

This edition is published for sale only in the United Kingdom and Eire.

© Marshall Cavendish International (Asia) Pte Ltd 2006
Originated and designed by Times Editions–Marshall Cavendish
An imprint of Marshall Cavendish International (Asia) Pte Ltd
1 New Industrial Road, Singapore 536196

Written by: Harlinah Whyte & Nicole Frank
Designer: Cynthia Ng
Picture researchers: Thomas Khoo & Joshua Ang

A CIP catalogue record for this book
is available from the British Library.

ISBN-10: 0 7496 7021 5
ISBN-13: 978 0 7496 7021 4

Printed in Malaysia

Franklin Watts is a division of Hachette Children's Books.

PICTURE CREDITS
A.N.A. Press Agency: 3 (bottom), 12, 45
Axiom Photographic Agency: 3 (centre), 5,
    27, 37, 39
BES Stock: 3 (top), 4, 6, 10, 20, 30, 31, 42
Haga Library: 26, 32 (both)
Hutchison Library: cover, 2, 8 (both),
    17 (top), 18, 28, 35, 36
Life File: 17 (bottom), 23, 24, 38, 41
Photobank Photolibrary: 1, 7, 11, 14, 15,
    19, 22, 40, 43
Liba Taylor: 29, 33
Topham Picturepoint: 9, 13, 16, 21, 34
Travel Ink: 25

Digital Scanning by Superskill Graphics Pte Ltd

Contents

Words that appear in the glossary are printed in **bold** the first time they occur in the text.

4

Welcome to Japan!

Japan is a country rich in history and tradition. Its culture dates back thousands of years. Today, the Japanese islands hold a **unique** blend of Eastern and Western cultures. The country is a leader in technology. Join us and explore the land, people and lifestyles of Japan!

Opposite: The streets of Tokyo are busy with activity.

Below: These Japanese children sip their favourite soft drinks, just like children in Western cultures.

The Flag of Japan

The Japanese flag is white with a large red circle in the middle. The circle represents the sun. The Japanese call their country *Nihon*, which means "source of the sun". Japan is also known as the "Land of the Rising Sun".

The Land

Japan sits in the Pacific Ocean off the northeastern coast of Asia. The four main islands of Japan – Honshu, Hokkaido, Shikoku and Kyushu – have breathtaking ocean views and beautiful mountains. The Kanto Plain, on the island of Honshu, is the largest area of flat land in Japan. Many large cities, including Japan's capital, Tokyo, are on the Kanto Plain.

Below: The Japanese Alps are popular with skiers in winter.

Mount Fuji

Mount Fuji is the tallest mountain in Japan at 3,776 metres. This inactive volcano has not erupted since 1707 and is one of the international symbols of Japan. While some admire Mount Fuji from afar, thousands of people undertake the challenge of climbing it. In winter and spring, the peak is covered with snow.

Climate

The climate of Japan varies widely. In the north, the winters are long and harsh. Sapporo, in the north, has an average winter temperature of -5° Celsius. Further south, the climate is comfortably warm. In Okinawa, the average winter temperature is 15° C.

Above: Maple trees turn bright shades of red, yellow and orange in the autumn.

Left: Cherry trees bloom for less than a week every year in Japan. Many people go to parks to see the blossoms.

Plants and Animals

More than 60 per cent of Japan is covered with forest. The trees grow on steep, remote mountains. This makes the trees difficult to chop down and allows them to survive. Japan is one of the most highly forested developed countries.

Japan is home to many unique animals such as the Asiatic brown bear. This bear lives on Honshu, Kyushu and Shikoku. Japan is also home to waterbirds, such as the crane.

Above: The Japanese macaque lives on Honshu, Shikoku and Kyushu. Bushy fur keeps this animal warm in winter.

History

Siberians were probably the first people to settle in Japan. Later, Chinese and Koreans moved there. Families, known as clans, fought for land. Leaders of clans were called "emperors", a title still used today.

Left: Many buildings were ruined during wars for land. The Todaiji Temple at Nara was completely destroyed and then rebuilt in a modern style of architecture.

The Heian Era and Civil War

Kyoto or Heian became the capital of Japan in 794. During the Heian Era, the Fujiwara clan held and lost power. Later, Minamoto Yoritomo became the military leader of Japan. Fighting continued and a **civil war** began. In the 1500s, Tokugawa Ieyasu united Japan. He expelled foreigners and banned his people from travelling. This **isolation** lasted more than 200 years.

Above: Buddhism, art and **samurai** culture were very popular in the city of Kamakura for hundreds of years. This picture was painted in the Kamakura period.

Ending Japanese Isolation

Foreigners returned to Japan in 1854 when American traders arrived, ending Japanese isolation. In 1868, Emperor Meiji took power. He **modernised** Japan and introduced railroads, public schools and a **constitution** to the country.

Japan at War

Japan's power grew steadily through the 1900s. The country fought and

Above: These Japanese navy officers are part of the Self Defence Force. Japan's post-World War II constitution says the country will not go to war again, but Japan still keeps a military force.

defeated many countries including China, Russia and Korea.

Japan entered World War II on 7 December 1941. On that day, it bombed the United States naval base at Pearl Harbor, Hawaii. The war lasted for nearly four more years. In 1945, the United States destroyed the cities of Hiroshima and Nagasaki with atomic bombs. Japan was devastated and finally surrendered.

Below: Emperor Hirohito was the longest reigning emperor in Japan's history. He ruled the country from 1926 until his death in 1989.

Murasaki Shikibu (978–1026)

Murasaki Shikibu wrote one of the most famous books in Japan, *The Tale of Genji*. It is a story about life in the Heian royal court.

Minamoto Yoritomo (1147–1199)

In 1192, Minamoto Yoritomo became the first **shogun** of Japan. He established a **feudal system** that lasted until the 1800s.

Above: This is a statue of Tokugawa Ieyasu. He founded the city of Tokyo.

Tokugawa Ieyasu (1543–1616)

In 1600, Tokugawa Ieyasu became the shogun of Japan. The Tokugawa clan ruled Japan for over 200 years.

Emperor Meiji (1852–1912)

In 1868, after a national revolution called the *Meiji Restoration*, Emperor Meiji became the head of a new **democratic** government. He helped modernise Japan.

Opposite: Emperor Meiji's birth name was Prince Musuhito. At 15, when he became emperor, he changed his name to Meiji.

Government and the Economy

Government

After World War II, Japan wrote a new constitution emphasising the ideas of peace and human rights. The constitution includes a section that says that Japan cannot go to war again.

The prime minister heads Japan's democratic government. He is assisted

Below: The National Diet Building is located in Tokyo.

Left: Elections are held for governors. Candidates travel through cities by bus or tram asking for support from the voters.

by members of the Diet, which is the national **legislature**, or law-making body, of Japan. The Diet is divided into two chambers — the House of Councillors and the House of Representatives. The Diet makes the national laws.

Japan is divided into forty-seven areas, called **prefectures**. Each prefecture has its own governor and officials. The officials are in charge of maintaining parks and school systems and providing health care.

Below: Every neighbourhood has a "police box", which is a miniature police station with one room. People go there for help or to report problems.

Economic Development

Selling products to other countries has made Japan an economic leader in the world. Japan makes many types of goods, such as cars, televisions, computers and cameras for **export**. It continues to spend a lot of money to develop new, high-quality products.

Japanese companies have also built factories in neighbouring South Korea, Hong Kong, Taiwan and Malaysia, where costs are lower.

Above: Japanese workers are loyal to their company and often work at the same company for many years. This woman makes printer ribbons at Hitachi Heavy Metals.

Energy

Most of Japan's energy comes from gas, oil and coal. Japan has also developed nuclear power stations, but these produce very dangerous waste products.

Agriculture

Rice is the staple food of the Japanese diet. It is expensive to produce, and costs more than foreign rice. In 1993, Japan was forced to import rice from other countries when its crops failed.

Below: It is time to harvest the crop. Farms in Japan are usually small.

People and Lifestyle

Who lives in Japan?

Japan has the tenth largest population in the world. Around 127 million people live there.

The original people of Japan are the **Ainu** (eye-noo). They are one of several minority groups. The Ainu lived in Japan before immigrants arrived from the Asian continent.

Below: These girls pose for a picture making a V with their fingers. This is a popular photo pose in Japan.

Types of Buildings

Large cities such as Tokyo, Osaka and Yokohama are home to over 75 per cent of the population. People live in low-rise buildings and work in medium-rise buildings.

Japanese Homes

Japanese homes are very small. People sleep on *futon* (foo-ton) bedding on the living room floor. In the morning, the futons are rolled up and stored in a cupboard.

Above: *Tatami* (tah-tah-mee) floors are common in Japan. They are made from tightly woven rice stalks and are very soft to walk on.

Belonging to a Group

In Japan, heavy value is placed on the ability to fit into a group. Groups are important in both work and social situations. They show that people can blend in and act together.

Growing Up

When a child starts going to school, he or she becomes part of a new group. Children are expected to fit in with others and not break any rules.

Above: A group of friends cools off during the summer. Group relationships are important to Japanese people.

Roles for Men and Women

Men in Japan work long hours with many late nights. They are expected to earn the money for their family.

When women get married, some of them give up their jobs. They stay at home and take care of the children. They also supervise their children's schoolwork. Today, there are more working women in Japan than women who do not work outside the home.

Below: Women have many responsibilities. In addition to caring for their children, they also handle the family money.

Education

The competition in Japanese schools is strong. Students have to pass difficult tests to enter each level. The most difficult exam is the university entrance exam. Some students take the exams many times before passing.

Left: These girls wear colourful graduation dresses. Students who go to top universities often work for the government or the best companies after graduation.

School Life

Students go to school 240 days a year, with a six-week holiday in the summer. They have lessons from Monday to Friday, and a half day on Saturday. Children are in charge of cleaning their schools.

Cram Schools

Cram schools help students prepare for university entrance exams. Some children attend these schools to make sure they pass their exams.

Above: Students must deal with the pressures of school from a young age. Doing well in exams is very important.

Shinto and Buddhism

The main religions in Japan are Shinto and Buddhism. *Shinto* (shin-to) means "ways of the gods". This religion began in Japan in **prehistoric** times. People go to Shinto shrines to ask the gods for help in hard times.

Buddhism was introduced to Japan in 522 CE. Buddhists believe that when someone dies, their soul lives on and comes back to life again and again.

Above: A Shinto table like this can be found in many Japanese homes. The cat with its raised paw is supposed to bring good luck.

This is called reincarnation. Most Japanese funerals are Buddhist.

Christianity

Only about 1 per cent of Japanese follow the Christian faith.

Left: Each year, numerous people visit this Great Buddha in Kamakura. Buddhists have a positive outlook on death. They believe that when a person dies, his or her soul is born again into a new being.

Language

Spoken Japanese

The spoken Japanese language is made up of simple sounds and grammar. Spoken Japanese is very difficult to learn and may take many years to master.

Left: You must have a great memory to learn Japanese. You need to know over three thousand written characters called **kanji** (kahn-jee) to read a newspaper!

Written Japanese

There are three systems of writing in Japanese – *kanji*, **hiragana** (hee-rah-gah-nah) and **katakana** (kah-tah-kah-nah). Kanji was adopted from Chinese culture, and it is the most difficult to learn.

Literature

Women wrote the first novels in Japan during the Heian Era. *The Tale of Genji* is the most famous of these.

Above: Books are very popular in Japan. During the twentieth century, Japanese writers Kawabata Yasunari and Oe Kenzaburo both won the Nobel Prize for Literature.

Arts

Crafts

In Japan, highly skilled craftspeople are called "living national treasures". The government pays these artists to teach their crafts to other people.

Painting

Older Japanese paintings focus on the events of everyday life and the passing of the seasons. Some families

Below: These Japanese crafts are bright and colourful. They are also fun to play with!

Above: This historic Japanese painting shows Westerners in Japan.

hang these long, painted scrolls in their homes. Today, modern art is also popular in Japan.

Calligraphy

Writing Japanese characters with brush and ink is called calligraphy. This specialised art is taught to schoolchildren.

Prints

Woodblock printing is one of Japan's most famous arts. Carving, painting and pressing the blocks onto paper results in beautiful prints.

Traditional Theatre

In Japanese theatre, the same stories are told again and again so the audience often knows what to expect.

Noh, Bunraku and Kabuki

Noh (no) is an ancient form of Japanese theatre based on religious stories. Actors chant their lines and move their bodies in slow motion. *Bunraku* (boon-rah-koo) mixes storytelling, puppetry and music.

Above: Noh theatre masks.

The puppets' mouths, eyes and eyebrows all move! ***Kabuki*** (kah-boo-kee) theatre is fun with lots of action. It is very exciting to watch.

Film, Television and Music

These popular arts originated in Western culture and have been adapted to suit Japanese tastes. Kurosawa Akira (*The Seven Samurai*) and Itami Juzo (*Tampopo*) are Japan's best-known filmmakers.

Leisure

Time to Relax

A popular hobby with Japanese women is *ikebana* (ee-keh-bah-nah), the art of flower arranging. These flower arrangements are displays of natural beauty.

The tea ceremony is an ancient **ritual** in Japan. The host serves green tea to guests and allows them to enjoy the simple pleasures of nature.

Below: This woman is practising ikebana. Each flower is placed very carefully.

Left: Pachinko (pah-cheen-ko) mixes the fun of pinball and slot machines. It is named for the sound the steel balls make in the machine — *pachin!*

Karaoke (kah-rah-oh-keh) is a favourite pastime in Japan. At special clubs, people sing along to recorded music. They read the song lyrics off television screens.

The Japanese also enjoy travelling within Japan and to other countries.

Sport

Baseball or *besuboru* (beh-soo-baw-roo) is the most popular team sport in Japan. Japan has two leagues, each with six teams. The Tokyo Giants is the name of the most popular team.

Left: Japanese people of all ages love baseball. Fifteen million citizens attend baseball games every year.

Traditional Japanese fighting and self-defence have made way for modern martial arts, such as ***karate*** (kah-rah-tay) and ***judo*** (joo-doh). Many martial arts competitions take place in Japan.

In 1993, the J-League, Japan's first professional football league, was created. J-League clothing and products fill stores trying to keep up with the demand from teenagers.

Above: In the Japanese sport of **kendo** (ken-doh), athletes fence with bamboo swords.

Gion Matsuri

The *Gion Matsuri* (gee-on-mah-tsoo-ree) festival takes place every year on 17 July. Originally, it was to ask the gods for protection from the plague, a killer disease. Now, the festival has become a traditional celebration.

Above: The Gion Matsuri festival began in 876 CE. These musicians ride through town on one of the many floats during the annual parade.

New Year's Day

The New Year, called *Shogatsu* (show-gah-tsoo), is the biggest festival of the year in Japan and lasts three days.

Bon Festival

During the *Bon* (bon) festival, people believe ghosts return to Earth. Floating candles and lanterns are placed on rivers to guide the ghosts back to heaven or hell. Many people return to their hometowns to clean their family graves during Bon.

Left: Children's Day, *Kodomo-no-hi* (koh-doh-moh-no-hee) is celebrated on 5 May. Banners, such as these, are hung outside Japanese homes. The carp is a symbol of bravery and strength.

Food

Japanese Meals

Japanese meals are very healthy. Rice is the basis of the Japanese diet – most people eat it at least twice a day. It is so important, in fact, that meals are called "morning rice", "noon rice" and "evening rice".

Little squares of vinegared rice and raw fish or egg wrapped in

Left: Few spices are used in Japanese cooking. The food is always fresh and presented in small dishes.

seaweed are called *sushi* (soo-shee).
Sushi is a popular lunch dish and
comes in many varieties.

Above: Pasta is a popular alternative to rice.

Foreign Influences

Through the years, Japan has adopted
dishes from other countries – even
hamburgers! The foods are changed,
however, to fit Japanese tastes. The
Japanese top their pizza with squid
and seaweed and use Japanese sauces
in other foreign dishes.

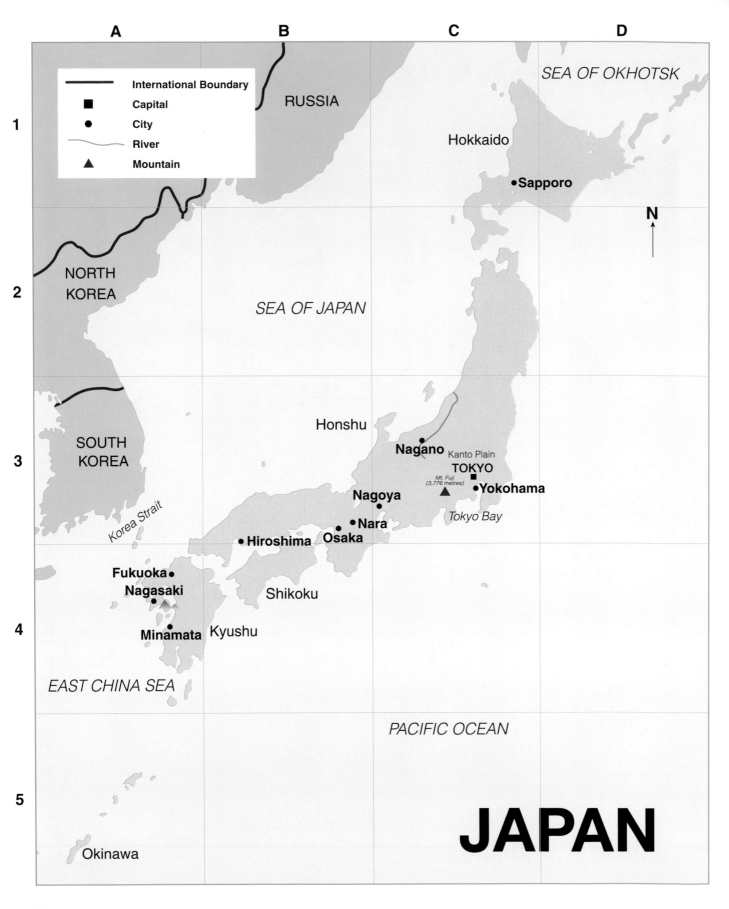

A   B   C   D

International Boundary
Capital
City
River
Mountain

1

RUSSIA

SEA OF OKHOTSK

Hokkaido

●Sapporo

N

NORTH
KOREA

2

SEA OF JAPAN

SOUTH
KOREA

3

Honshu

Nagano●

Kanto Plain

TOKYO

Mt. Fuji
(3,776 metres) ▲

●**Yokohama**

Korea Strait

●**Nagoya**

●**Nara**

Tokyo Bay

●**Hiroshima**

Osaka●

Fukuoka●

Nagasaki

Shikoku

●
Minamata

Kyushu

4

EAST CHINA SEA

PACIFIC OCEAN

5

JAPAN

Okinawa

42

Above: The majestic splendour of Mount Fuji.

East China Sea A4

Fukuoka A4

Hiroshima B3
Hokkaido C1
Honshu C2

Kanto Plain C3
Korea Strait A3
Kyushu B4

Minamata A4
Mount Fuji C3

Nagasaki A4
Nagoya C3
Nara B3
North Korea A2

Okinawa A5
Osaka B3

Pacific Ocean C5

Russia B1

Sapporo C1
Sea of Japan B2

Shikoku B4
South Korea A3

Tokyo C3

Tokyo Bay C3

Yokohama C3

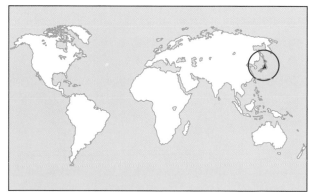

Quick Facts

Official Name	Japan (Nihon)
Capital	Tokyo
Official Language	Japanese
Population	127 million
Land Area	374,646 square kilometres
Largest Islands	Hokkaido, Honshu, Kyushu, Shikoku
Highest Point	Mount Fuji (3,776 metres)
Main Religions	Buddhism, Shinto
Major Festivals	New Year's Day, Children's Day, Bon, Gion Matsuri
Major Cities	Tokyo, Osaka, Yokohama
Ethnic Groups	Japanese and Ainu (99.2 per cent)
	Korean (0.6 per cent)
	Others (0.2 per cent)
National Flower	Cherry blossom
National Flag	White with a large red circle (representing the sun) in the centre
Currency	Japanese Yen (¥141.077 = 1 Euro in May 2006)

Opposite: American characters, such as Superman, are popular with Japanese children.

Index